THE
SNOW BABY

The Arctic Childhood
of Admiral Robert E. Peary's
Daring Daughter

KATHERINE KIRKPATRICK

Holiday House / New York

For my own adventuresome daughters,
Hannah and Gwen

The images of snowflakes on the jacket and throughout the book
are from *Snowflakes in Photographs* by W. A. Bentley (New York:
Dover Publications, 2000).

The photographs in this book were reproduced as tritones in silver, blue, and black.
The silver ink was used to emulate the affect of a platinum print, a type of photographic print
popular until the 1920's. Platinum prints were prized for their great range of subtle tonal variations
of silvery grays. The blue was used to convey the look and feel of ice and snow.

Inuit words and names in this text are spelled according to the way
Marie Peary spelled them in her published writings.

Library of Congress Cataloging-in-Publication Data
Kirkpatrick, Katherine.
The snow baby : the Arctic childhood of Admiral Robert E. Peary's Daring Daughter /
by Katherine Kirkpatrick.— 1st ed.
p.   cm.
ISBN-13: 978-0-8234-1973-9 (hardcover)
ISBN-10: 0-8234-1973-8 (hardcover)
1. Peary, Marie Ahnighito, 1893–1978—Childhood and youth.   2. Peary, Robert E.
(Robert Edwin), 1856–1920—Family.   3. Arctic regions—Biography.   4. Washington
(D.C.)—Biography.   5. Children—Arctic regions—Biography.   6. Children—Washington
(D.C.)—Biography.   7. Explorers—Family relationships.   I. Title.
   CT275.K5934   2007
   910'922—dc22   2006002016

One of Peary's "king" dogs

Contents

	Map	v
Chapter One	The Snow Baby	1
Chapter Two	A Life of Contrasts	6
Chapter Three	Moving the Iron Mountain	10
Chapter Four	Adventures on the *Windward*	16
Chapter Five	Winter on the Ice-Locked Ship	22
Chapter Six	Reunions and Farewells	28
Chapter Seven	Eagle Island	35
Chapter Eight	The Victory Tour	39
	Afterword	46
	Bibliography	48
	Source Notes	48
	Acknowledgments and Picture Credits	49
	Index	50

Josephine Peary and baby Marie

Notes on Peary's Expeditions

For the majority of his Arctic expeditions, Admiral Peary sailed from Newfoundland and disembarked at a predesignated place. The following summer, the ship would bring supplies and pick up expedition members. As Peary's views on how he might reach the North Pole evolved, he changed his expedition bases. In the earliest journeys he used Etah, Greenland, as his starting point. In later trips, he camped on Ellesmere Island, at Cape Sabine, and then at Fort Conger. During each expedition, Peary stopped at Etah and took aboard Inuit workers. He relied on them to make clothing, hunt for food, and drive dogsleds. In Peary's last two journeys, his ship the *Roosevelt* became his base. He brought it to a point he named Cape Sheridan, along the northern coast of Ellesmere Island, where it stayed for the remainder of the expeditions.

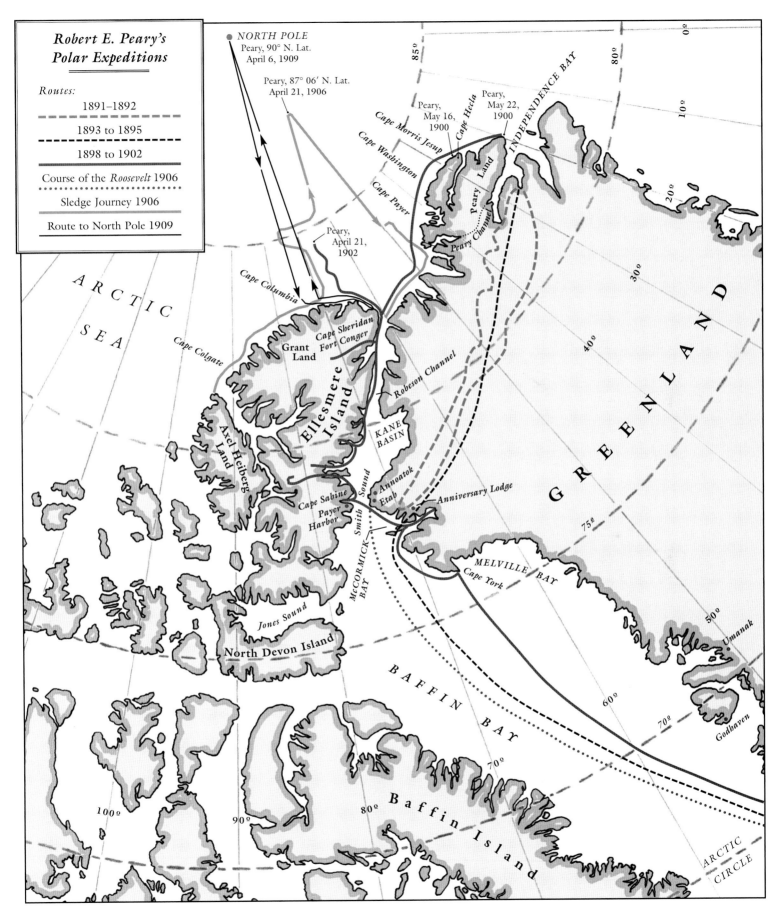

Robert E. Peary's
Polar Expeditions

Routes:

1891–1892

1893 to 1895

1898 to 1902

Course of the *Roosevelt* 1906

Sledge Journey 1906

Route to North Pole 1909

NORTH POLE
Peary, 90° N. Lat.
April 6, 1909

Peary, 87° 06′ N. Lat.
April 21, 1906

Peary,
May 16,
1900

Peary, May 22,
1900

Cape Hecla

Cape Morris Jesup

INDEPENDENCE BAY

Cape Washington

Peary Land

Cape Payer

Peary Channel

Peary, April 21,
1902

Cape Columbia

Cape Colgate

ARCTIC

SEA

Cape Sheridan
Fort Conger

Grant
Land

Ellesmere
Island

Robeson Channel

GREENLAND

KANE
BASIN

Axel Heiberg
Land

Cape Sabine
Payer
Harbor

Smith Sound

Annoatok
Etah

Anniversary Lodge

75°

North Devon Island

Jones Sound

McCORMICK
BAY

MELVILLE BAY
Cape York

BAFFIN

BAY

Umanak

Godhaven

50°

60°

70°

100°

90°

80°

70°

70°

60°

B a f f i n   I s l a n d

ARCTIC
CIRCLE

85°

80°

0°

10°

20°

30°

40°

1 minute of latitude = 1 nautical mile, or about 1.151 statute miles.   60 minutes per degree of latitude = 60 nautical miles, or about 69.05 statute miles.

Marie, age seven, in kapetah

"Whenever people had exclaimed at my being 'The Snowbaby' and had made rather a fuss over me, Mother would explain to me later that I must be very proud of having a father who could make us so comfortable in a frozen land that even a small baby could live and be well and strong. As for myself, it was a piece of good fortune for me that I happened to have been that baby."

Marie Ahnighito Peary

Chapter One
The Snow Baby

In the far north of Greenland, at the edge of an icy bay, in a house covered with tar paper against the Arctic cold, a baby girl was born. Outside, winds roared and pushed the snow into towering drifts. Masses of ice groaned against each other. The frozen landscape sparkled in the brilliant sunshine. The date was September 12, 1893. The baby's parents named her Marie Ahnighito (ah-nee-gheé-toe) Peary.

News of her birth in this far place would in time spread around the globe. Marie's mother, Josephine "Jo" Diebitsch Peary, who came from a refined and educated family in Washington, D.C., had shocked Americans by accompanying her husband, the legendary explorer and U.S. naval officer, Lieutenant Robert E. Peary, to the Arctic. "She did this with no idea of being a

Anniversary Lodge, Marie's birthplace in 1893

heroine or making herself famous," Marie Peary later wrote of her mother. "She simply felt that her place was with her husband."

The house where Marie was born served as headquarters for Peary's 1893–1895 expedition. Peary named the house "Anniversary Lodge" because, several years before the house was built, he and Jo had spent their first wedding anniversary at this location. Though the house was small, its two large rooms gave good shelter. One room was for the Pearys and the nurse who delivered Marie, Mrs. Susan J. Cross, who had come with them from America. In the second room lived the other twelve members of the party. Each bed, enclosed by a curtain, was built four and a half feet off the cold ground.

The family lived among the Smith Sound Inuit, who helped Marie's father in exchange for goods, such as guns, knives, sewing needles, and wood for harpoons. Like the Inuit, Peary and his party dressed in layers of animal skins and furs and traveled by dogsled. They ate Inuit foods of

Lieutenant Robert E. and Josephine Peary as newlyweds, 1888

seal, caribou, and musk ox, as well as their own canned goods. Peary employed Inuit to hunt for his party, make clothes, and help guide his explorations. The news of Marie's birth caused great excitement among the Inuit, who came to see the blonde, blue-eyed baby. According to Peary, the Inuit wondered if the fair-skinned child was fully human or created from snow. They called her Ah-poo Mickaninny: "Snow Baby." Journalists all over the world popularized the nickname.

When Marie was six weeks old, Mrs. Peary wrapped her in a caribou skin bag, furs, and an American flag, then carried her outdoors so she could see the sunlight glisten over the snow. To the proud and patriotic father, who took the baby's photograph, this display of the flag put his own mark on the cold, distant land. The sun would soon disappear: the long "Great Night" of the Arctic winter was about to begin. Marie stayed indoors for the next four months. In all this time, the only light she saw was the round, faint glow of lamplight.

Every day, Marie enjoyed a bath as her mother

Marie's first trip outdoors

sponged her with warm water heated on an oil stove. Afterward, Marie was allowed to roll naked on the soft caribou skins on her bed. Peary had packed plenty of tea and biscuits; perhaps one of those biscuits was Marie's first solid food. Outside the lodge, a dozen or two of Peary's sled dogs, who slept burrowed in the snow, sometimes howled together, making a mournful song.

Living in such a remote place, in the total ab-

Josephine Peary holding baby Marie

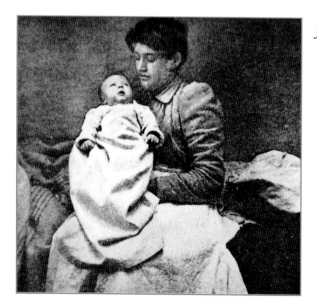

The Arctic night

Josephine Peary in a hunting outfit, 1891

Journal, she praised her husband's skills at making a home so comfortable in the far north that even a lady could live there without complaints. She only wished he'd remembered a broom so she could sweep the house.

During the Arctic winter, Peary needed to keep his American expedition members almost constantly busy outside to maintain their physical fitness and to prevent them from becoming depressed. The parties hunted by moonlight, experimented with sled designs, and perfected cooking stoves and other equipment they'd later use on their polar journeys.

In February, the long darkness ended. Peary wrote, "When the earliest ray of the returning sun pierced through the window of our tiny room, [Marie] reached for the golden bar as other children reach for a beautiful toy." Soon Marie was ready to go outside in the clothes that an Inuit woman, Ahnighito, her namesake, had

sence of sunlight, would have been a frightening existence for most American women. But Josephine Peary had already experienced an Arctic winter on one of her husband's earlier expeditions. She'd learned to hunt caribou and fox. While afloat in a rowboat, she'd even shot at large attacking walruses. In her book *My Arctic*

Marie reaches for the beam of light.

made for her. She wore a fox skin coat topped by a caribou skin hood, with warm foxtails sewn about the wrists and hood openings. Her caribou skin trousers and fur-lined boots were sewn in one piece. Marie rode in a box mounted on a little sled while her mother guided the dogs.

Two Inuit children visited Marie. One was a twelve-year-old girl named Eklayashoo, nicknamed Miss Bill by the Pearys. Marie later called her Billy Bah because she couldn't pronounce either of her names. Marie's other companion was six-year-old Nipsangwah, also called Koodlooktoo, which means "the little orphan boy."

When Koodlooktoo was a baby, his father was killed by a walrus, and his mother had died soon afterward. Matthew "Matt" Henson, Peary's personal aide, and his most loyal and

Marie with sled dog puppies

capable expedition member, adopted Koodlooktoo during the years they spent in Greenland. Henson washed and scrubbed the boy, cut his long hair short, and dressed him in a suit made of cloth and fur from the party's supplies.

As spring turned to summer, and the ice receded, Mrs. Peary sometimes spread a caribou skin on the warm gravel bank near the house for ten-month-old Marie to crawl on. Marie tumbled joyfully with sled dog puppies. She laughed when her mother gave her brilliant purple flowers that carpeted the hillside nearby. Living now in constant sunshine, Marie grew quickly. Her eyes shone, and her cheeks took on a healthy glow. Her father said she was like a tulip or hyacinth bulb, kept in the dark all winter, quickly expanding and blossoming when placed in a window.

While Marie grew strong and thrived in the Arctic, her father faced many setbacks with his expedition. When there was enough daylight to travel, Peary set out with a party of seven American team members, five Inuit, twelve sleds (also

Nipsangwah, or Koodlooktoo, "the little orphan boy," around 1894

known as sledges), and some ninety dogs, attempting to cross the polar ice cap of Greenland. Two team members became ill and turned back early; the rest of the party was caught in raging snowstorms. Peary and his men were exhausted and suffered from snow blindness. In the harsh weather, most of the dogs died. Peary gave up his explorations and returned to the lodge.

Despite this failure, Peary did make a shorter, more successful trip that summer. Inuit near the Cape York region took Peary to see three giant meteorites. Peary carved the initial "P" on one of them. He hoped to return later to claim all three.

In late July, Inuit messengers came to tell Peary that they had spotted a black-hulled, yellow-masted whaler in nearby waters. It was Peary's ship, the *Falcon,* which his supporters back in the United States had sent to bring Peary and his party home. Peary had not expected to see the ship for another summer; it had come a year early because his wife's family had been concerned for her and the baby.

Peary, already planning a new expedition in

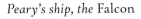

Peary's ship, the Falcon

the spring of 1895, decided to remain in Greenland. All but two of his party, Matt Henson and Hugh Lee, chose to return to the United States. Mrs. Peary wanted to stay with her husband, but he persuaded her to leave on the *Falcon.* Marie's nurse, as well as the expedition's doctor, would be leaving on the ship. Peary did not want his little daughter to be in Greenland without a doctor. The *Falcon* would also take the Inuit girl Billy Bah to spend a year in the United States.

The ship departed on August 26, sailing beneath the gleaming glacier of Smith Sound. With Marie in her arms, Mrs. Peary waved until her husband was no longer visible. She did not know when she would see him again. Occasionally, the couple might have an opportunity to send letters through whaling ships that visited the Arctic.

Though Peary was saddened to see his wife and baby leave, he looked forward to future explorations. With each new journey on the ice, he learned techniques that brought him closer to achieving his ultimate goal: being the first man to reach the North Pole. Yet he wondered if Marie would recognize him when he saw her next. "Will she always be as bright and quick and strong and healthy as she is now?" he wrote in his journal. "What will be her fate in life, happy or unhappy?"

Safe in her mother's embrace, little Marie, now eleven months old, sailed off to a land of green trees and grass—a whole new world for the Snow Baby.

Chapter Two
A Life of Contrasts

The *Falcon* docked in Philadelphia. Marie, her mother, and Billy Bah made their way to the station to catch a train to Washington, D.C. As they stood waiting, an engine roared past, and Billy Bah, who thought it was a man-eating animal, clung to Mrs. Peary in terror.

Together one-year-old Marie and twelve-year-old Billy Bah experienced city life for the first time. Horse-drawn carriages clattered by. The girls' feet trod in soft grass. They saw leafy maple trees and towering four-story buildings, and smelled the black smoke that poured from tall smokestacks.

"That was part of the fascination of my childhood, the sudden contrasts and the constant change," Marie later wrote.

Billy Bah was Marie's companion during the year they lived with Marie's grandmother and aunt, the Diebitsches, in Washington, D.C. In her memoir, Marie mentions that Billy Bah called houses "igloos" and horses "big dogs." Marie's mother dressed Billy Bah in underwear, a woolen dress, stockings, and shoes. She reluctantly allowed herself to be bathed, though she refused to brush her teeth.

Marie and Billy Bah lived in a two-story wooden house that was far larger, warmer, and brighter than the homes they'd known. Gaslight lamps lit the rooms. Servants tended fires in

Eklayashoo, also known as "Billy Bah," around age twelve, during the year she lived in Washington, D.C.

marble fireplaces. By contrast, in Billy Bah's family igloo, light came from chunks of oily seal blubber placed in soapstone lamps with moss wicks. Over the lamps hung small soapstone pots, in which snow was melted for drinking water. At the Diebitsches' house, abundant clear water—that didn't taste of seal—spurted out of faucets as if by magic.

The Diebitsch house, 2014 Twelfth Street, Washington, D.C., 1908

Marie and Billy Bah slept in their own bedrooms at the top of a carpeted stairway. Billy Bah was lonely for her faraway family and their snug igloo of rocks and snow. She slept nestled with the Diebitsches' kitten for company. Yet in their new surroundings, both girls found plenty to interest and delight them. Downstairs in the family's spacious parlor, Billy Bah rolled around with Hector, Mrs. Peary's big, shaggy Saint Bernard. Marie, wearing a white lace dress and bonnet that covered her blonde curls, tugged at the gentle dog's fur. Aunt "Tante" Marie, Marie's namesake, played the piano for the girls and sang to them.

Marie's uncle Emil visited frequently. He always brought along a smile and a joke; Marie adored him. Other callers, women in flowing dresses and plumed hats, spoke in a language that, at first, must have sounded strange to Billy Bah and little Marie. For Marie's grandmother Magdelena "Maria" Diebitsch, whom Marie called Grossy (short for *Grossmutter*), chatted with her friends in her native tongue, German. Her husband, Hans Herman Diebitsch, also an immigrant to America, had translated languages at the Smithsonian Institution.

Both of Marie's grandfathers had passed away before her birth. Marie's father, called Bertie by his family, was an only child and grew up with his widowed mother, Mary Wiley Peary, in Portland, Maine. A frail and sickly woman, she completely devoted herself to her spirited son; to his embarrassment, she even moved with her son to nearby Brunswick, when he was accepted to Bowdoin College on a scholarship. Mary Peary died when Marie was seven. But Grossy, Marie's grandmother in Washington, D.C., played a major role throughout Marie's childhood, and Marie always retained a special fondness for her.

Marie's parents met at a dancing school in Washington, D.C., during her father's first appointment as a naval engineer. Josephine Diebitsch possessed a quiet strength and independence; almost at once, the dashing redhead Bertie Peary decided he wanted to marry her. "Luck was surely with [Robert E. Peary] when he chose his wife and she chose him," Marie

The Diebitsch family, clockwise from the bottom left: Jo Peary, Grossy, Emil, and Marie (Mayde)

later wrote of her parents. Marie believed it was her mother's steadfast support and devotion to her father that made his accomplishments in the Arctic possible. While he never imagined she'd give birth to their first child in the Arctic, Peary saw that Jo was a woman who understood his great ambition of traveling to places no man had seen before. The Diebitsch family supported Peary's Arctic work, and Jo's brother, Emil Diebitsch, even accompanied Peary on several Arctic voyages.

The Diebitsches happily made Billy Bah a part of the family. Billy Bah had to learn to sit at the table and to eat cooked foods during appointed mealtimes. In the Arctic, her own people sat on the floor and ate whenever they were hungry. Though Billy Bah never complained about the food, when she returned to Greenland a year later, Peary reported she hungrily bit into a great slab of raw meat as if it were the first good meal she'd eaten in a long time. The diet she'd grown up with had also helped keep her strong and warm in the Arctic.

One day Billy Bah left Marie's toys and an embroidered carriage blanket of Mrs. Peary's on a city street, and when she came back for them, she was shocked to discover someone had taken them. Inuit people never touched anything that was not offered or that did not belong to them.

Mrs. Peary taught Billy Bah to sew, and Billy Bah took pleasure in making clothes for her doll. She eagerly collected swatches of material to take back to Greenland. Mrs. Peary gave Billy Bah a trunk for her things. Mrs. Peary wrote, "Her trunk was a regular Noah's Ark. A bit of everything that was given to her during her stay was always carefully put into it."

At Christmastime, Grossy decorated a tree

Billy Bah (center) with her family in Greenland around 1891–1893

with ribbons, sparkling glass ornaments, and scores of tiny glowing candles. Tantalizing aromas of stollen, a traditional German Christmas cake; pastries; and roasting meats wafted through the house. After the family's celebration and exchange of gifts, without a word, Billy Bah carried her presents to her room. Seeing Billy Bah climb the stairs, Mrs. Peary feared the occasion was too unfamiliar for Billy Bah to enjoy completely. But when she checked on her later, she found Billy Bah happily playing with her new toys, smiling and singing to herself.

That first winter in Washington, D.C., Mrs. Peary raised money to bring her husband and his party back to the United States. The *Falcon*, Mrs. Peary learned, had been wrecked in a storm on its return journey to St. John's, Newfoundland. Mrs. Peary met with many wealthy people, seeking funds to charter another ship, the *Kite*. She approached Morris K. Jesup, the president of the American Museum of Natural History in New York. Jesup was to become Peary's main benefactor.

The following summer, the *Kite* steamed from St. John's, Newfoundland, to Greenland, carrying among other passengers Marie's uncle Emil and Billy Bah. Mrs. Peary had also planned to go on the ship, along with Marie, now nearly two. But the Diebitsches, privately fearing that Peary might not have survived his latest expedition, convinced her to stay at home.

Peary, Matt Henson, and Hugh Lee nearly *had* died. Their journey of April 1895 had been

Marie, around age two

even more disastrous than the expedition of the previous spring. As the Americans, three Inuit, and sixty sled dogs set out toward the polar cap, they encountered violent gales and snowstorms. Lee's sledge was smashed. Ice buried the food Peary had left in storage caches along their route. Many dogs died or had to be killed to feed other dogs. The men, too, were close to starvation, so Peary gave up the mission. By the time the men returned to their camp at Anniversary Lodge, only one dog was still alive.

Peary concluded that he would need to find another route to begin crossing the ice cap, and that next time he would depart from a point much farther north. To do this, he'd need to raise money for a sturdier, more powerful ship. So Peary returned home to Washington, D.C., to his lively and engaging two-year-old daughter and his very patient and steadfast wife.

Chapter Three
Moving the Iron Mountain

During the next two years, Peary served as a naval engineer in Brooklyn, New York. Marie came to know him as both adoring and stern. When Marie disobeyed her father by leaving playthings on the floor of his office, he took

Josephine Peary in the Peary family's Brooklyn apartment, 1895–1896. Note the polar bear rug.

away some of her favorite toys and kept them for months. Yet Marie's father often read to her and told her stories of "Snowland." Marie always remembered the tale of her father's transporting a caboose to Etah, Greenland. The former train car, which was missing its wheels, served as a ready-made house for Peary. There the caboose sat, a bright red curiosity among the igloos and tents of warm skins.

For weeks at a time, Marie saw little of her father because of his frequent cross-country lecture tours. Nearly all of the money Peary earned went toward his future Arctic expeditions.

Three-year-old Marie, now wearing a proper long Victorian dress, bonnet, dark stockings, and button-up boots, probably attended a few of her father's lectures. To add excitement to his presentations, Peary hired the ever-faithful Matt Henson to wear (and perspire in) thick furs, brandish a whip, and race through the crowd onto the stage with six sled dogs. If the presentation went on too long, the dogs would grow restless and start to howl.

Peary's fund-raising efforts took many other forms. While in the Arctic, he had collected furs, ivory tusks, animals, and birds that a taxidermist on the ship prepared. These were sold to museums or presented to Peary's supporters. He sometimes sold live animals to zoos; once he brought back a pair of snarling polar bear cubs named Polaris and Cassiopeia. But Peary's greatest fundraising effort was the retrieval of a thirty-four-ton iron meteorite from Cape York, Greenland.

Marie, around age four, poses as a typical child of her era.

tists from the American Museum of Natural History, as well as Marie, now nearly four years old, and Mrs. Peary.

The great brown stones had split from a single flaming mass. According to Inuit legend, the evil spirit Tornarsuk hurled a woman, her dog, and her tent out of the sky. The "woman" stone had resembled a woman seated at her sewing. But over time, Inuit had chipped pieces out of the great iron stones to make knives and spear points, altering the meteorites' shapes.

Peary saw no reason why he shouldn't take the meteorites from Greenland. According to him, the Inuit no longer needed the iron meteorites because they could now trade for metal knife blades.

The Peary family boarded a three-masted schooner, the *Hope*, in August of 1897. Marie and her nanny, Laura, spent much of their time on deck, watching the seals, gulls, and occasional

The Inuit referred to this meteorite as the "tent" because its shape, jutting out of the ground, appeared triangular, like one of their dwellings. It was the largest of the three meteorites Peary discovered near the Cape York region. Peary had already brought back the two smaller meteorites, but his attempts during several different trips to the region to secure the "tent" had failed. On his final try, in 1897, confident he would succeed with stronger jacks and a more powerful vessel, Peary invited an audience to accompany him. The group included scien-

Marie at the helm of the Hope, *1897*

long-toothed whales called narwhals. Every day the air grew colder. The *Hope* zigzagged through a labyrinth of ice floes. When they steamed within the Arctic Circle, sunlight shone both day and night, and Marie resisted her mother's attempts to put her to bed. At night, Mrs. Peary wedged one of her husband's black felt hats into a porthole to darken their tiny stateroom.

When they reached North Greenland, Peary made a stop at Etah to visit the Inuit community. Marie stood at the rail to greet people in skin kayaks coming out to meet the ship. The Inuit were curious about the Snow Baby, whom they

hadn't seen for three years. They touched her curly blonde hair and giggled in surprise at Marie's height; she was so much taller than their children of the same age.

One of the first visitors to the ship was Billy Bah. Fourteen years old now and married, Billy Bah still eagerly played dolls with Marie. Billy Bah brought Marie a sealskin bag full of tiny ivory figures of people and animals, which she'd carved from walrus tusks. Marie's friend Koodlooktoo also came on board with a gift, a bag of ivory beads.

During this all-day party, the ship's cook handed out steaming mugs of tea and coffee to the Inuit visitors. On the forward deck, the Inuit gathered around Matt Henson, a great favorite of theirs. They admired his dark skin and considered him one of their own. He'd been the only

An iceberg in Etah, Greenland. Note the small figures and kayakers at the base of the iceberg.
(photo by Donald MacMillan)

Matthew
"Matt" Henson

one of Peary's men to learn their language, Inuktitut. In the sailors' quarters, the gramophone played constantly. The Inuit had never heard recorded music and believed that the gramophone was magic.

Peary chose Inuit workers to help retrieve the meteorite. They remained on the ship with their families; Koodlooktoo was among this group. Then the *Hope* set off to the place in Melville Bay that Peary had named Meteorite Island. To reach it, the ship would have to pass through a high-walled channel that was scarcely wider than the length of the ship. It was now the second week of August. Soon, thick ice would seal off the Bay. Peary knew that he only had a few weeks to try to secure the meteorite before leaving the Arctic again.

Approaching the island, the *Hope* headed through a snowstorm. Winds howled. Marie was seasick. After the storm passed, and the ship had anchored, Peary and his men prepared a space inside the hull to hold the meteorite. He lined the cavity with rocks and lumber. The crew worked for five days and nights, through snow and fog. They built an eighteen-foot bridge of steel rails joining the ship to the land. Using jacks, winches, and steel cables, the men lifted the meteorite into a timber cart, which would transport the meteorite, inch by inch, over the rails onto the ship.

While the men struggled to move the meteorite, Marie and the Inuit children built snow

Marie (left), nearly four, with friends on the Hope. *Marie holds Inuit dolls.*

Marie with Inuit children, during her trip to Greenland in 1897

houses on shore. Koodlooktoo and his friend Minik set out to trap birds for the ship's taxidermist. Minik caught a hawk and a snowy owl, and both boys were awarded pocketknives.

Before the attempt to hoist the meteorite by jacks into the *Hope*, Peary draped an American flag over it. He held Marie in his arms and gave her a little bottle of wine to break against the meteorite. Many years later, in her memoir, *The Snowbaby's Own Story*, she wrote: "I can still remember how excited I felt as Dad lifted me up and said: 'Now, my little girl, smash your bottle on the meteorite and say "I christen thee Ahnighito."'"

As the "great monster" hung in chains over the deck, ready to be lowered into the hull, a sailor raised the American flag to the top of a mast. Other sailors dismantled the bridge, the fog cleared, and the sun shone against a blue sky. Within hours, a furious gale descended. Afraid that the *Hope* would capsize, Peary and his men worked hard to lower the meteorite firmly into the hold.

Though the storm ended the next day, ice floes now blocked passage out of the bay. The captain drove the ship's wooden bow into the frozen sea, blow after blow. Finally, the ship wedged a path through the ice. Immediately after the ship passed through, the floes closed together again.

Before voyaging back to America, Peary made a stop on Bowdoin Bay to drop off his Inuit workers. Marie's parents took her to see the place of her birth. She picked bright purple, yellow,

The Ahnighito meteorite, hoisted into Peary's ship, the Hope

and white wildflowers on the spot where Anniversary Lodge had once stood. The lodge had burned down in a fire.

When the *Hope* set sail, five of the Inuit group, including Koodlooktoo's friend Minik and Billy Bah's parents, made an expedition of their own and remained on the ship with Peary. Asked by Franz Boas, an anthropologist at the American Museum of Natural History, to bring back one Inuit to learn from, Peary enlisted a whole group of volunteers. Peary promised he'd return them to Greenland within a year, with material goods that would benefit their people. Sadly, soon after reaching New York, all but two of the group died from illnesses that they had not developed resistance to.

During the *Hope*'s journey to New York, Peary directed the captain to make stops at several Danish settlements in South Greenland so scientists on board could collect fossils. At Umanak, Marie's dolls, with real hair and eyes that opened and closed, intrigued the Danish children. Marie, in turn, was fascinated by their rag dolls, with hair made of seaweed and dressed in colorful red-and-black costumes. As a parting gesture, Marie and one of the Danish girls exchanged dolls.

On September 12, Marie woke delighted to see her mother standing near her bed with a birthday cake. Later that day, the Pearys and expedition members gave Marie many gifts, including sealskin mittens and slippers and an eiderdown quilt. Captain Sam Bartlett blew four loud blasts on the ship's horn, Marie wrote, "to let all the seals and walrus and polar bears within hearing know that the Snow Baby was four years old that day."

After this happy occasion, the *Hope* sailed through another fierce gale. As winds howled above deck, Marie's father furiously worked below to adjust the meteorite's position so that the ship would stabilize. After the storm ended, fog still made the voyage perilous. Because of the magnetic pull from the meteorite's iron, the ship's compasses were useless. But Captain Bartlett skillfully brought the vessel into New York Harbor.

Little Marie was apparently unruffled by these stormy events. She remarked that her journey to "Snowland" had been great fun. When the family boarded a train to Washington, D.C., she was eager to return home, she said, because the dolls she'd left there missed her, and she missed them, too. Wouldn't it be a lovely surprise for them to meet their new "Eskimo" doll companion?

The meteorite stayed in the Brooklyn Naval Yard for two years. Eventually a barge carried the mass of iron up the East River to a pier at Fiftieth Street, on New York City's Upper East Side. From there, it was placed on a cart and pulled by twenty-eight horses to the American Museum of Natural History. The total payment to the Peary family for the three Cape York meteorites was $40,000—perhaps a million dollars by today's standards.

Chapter Four
Adventures on the *Windward*

In July 1898, when Marie was nearly five, she said good-bye to her father, who was departing for the Arctic again. From a pier, Marie and her mother waved while Peary's ship, the *Windward*, steamed out of New York Harbor. "Keep smiling as long as your father can see you!" Mrs. Peary told Marie, holding back her own tears.

This time, the *Windward* would return without Peary, because he planned to be away from his family for up to five years. He'd received an extended leave from the Navy to pursue his dream of reaching the North Pole. He took with him a silk American flag that Mrs. Peary had sewn as a good-bye present.

Though she deeply missed her father, Marie was excited because her mother was going to have a baby. In January 1899, Josephine Peary

Francine Peary, Marie's sister, was born in Washington, D.C., while her father was in the Arctic.

gave birth to a girl, Francine. Marie delighted in her newborn sister, attended kindergarten, and with her vivid imagination, dreamed of "marvelous plans for the future," which centered on "my new playmate and my large family of dolls."

That summer, the Diebitsch family rented a house on the beach at Atlantic City, New Jersey. Marie waded in the water at the beach and built sand castles with little Francine at her side. But then, at only seven months of age, Francine tragically came down with a sudden illness, possibly diphtheria, and, to the family's deep sorrow, died. Marie was heartbroken.

Earlier that month, Peary's ship, the *Windward*, had been sent back to Greenland by Peary's financial backers, collectively known as the Peary Arctic Club. The ship carried supplies and a letter from Peary's wife that announced Francine's birth. By the time Peary received the letter, Francine's death had already taken place.

When the *Windward* returned to the United States in the fall, it brought Mrs. Peary and Marie the news that Peary had lost nearly all his toes due to frostbite. After surgery, only the little toe of each foot remained. Only thirty-seven days after the injury, and though still suffering, Peary made another thwarted attempt at reaching the Pole.

By now, Mrs. Peary decided that it was time for her husband to come home. Morris Jesup, the president of the Peary Arctic Club, agreed. Peary's wealthy benefactors were also having doubts about Peary. Newspapers were calling him a "weather-

Morris K. Jesup,
president of the
Peary Arctic Club

beaten old fanatic." Though Jesup and Mrs. Peary knew it would not be easy to convince the proud explorer to give up his quest, together they worked out a plan. The following summer, the *Windward* was scheduled to take supplies again to Peary. Jesup arranged for Mrs. Peary and Marie to sail on the ship for Greenland.

On a hot July day in 1900, six-year-old Marie and Mrs. Peary boarded the *Windward* in Sydney, on Cape Breton, Nova Scotia. At first, Marie regarded the *Windward* as a "black sea monster." Filthy coal dust encrusted nearly every surface. The winches hoisting up provisions screeched. Captain Sam Bartlett, a large man with a limp, a red face, and a black beard, barked out orders to the sailors in a thundering voice. But Marie, like her father, relished adventure and had a way of pushing her fears aside.

When she saw the twinkle in his eye, Marie grew to like Captain Sam. The feeling was mutual. Captain Sam gave Marie a kitten and made a swing so Marie could watch the happenings on deck without getting in the sailors' way.

"Little Miss Peary is the pet of the trip," wrote one of the crew members in a letter that was later published in a newspaper. "I am teaching her how to signal [Morse code] and she has already learned the alphabet. We have great fun with her. She wears boy's clothing altogether and is as bright as a button."

Marie and her mother shared a tiny cabin. Staying in a nearby cabin with her husband was Martha Percy, wife of the ship's steward, "Old Charlie" Percy. Mrs. Percy was employed to be a nanny for Marie and a maid for her mother. As it was summertime, Marie was surprised to see the

Marie, age seven, on the Windward

Charles "Old Charlie" Percy, steward of Peary's ship, the Windward

By the end of the voyage's first week, a chilly, dense fog descended on the vessel. Captain Sam sounded the ship's loud whistle. Sailors at the bow and in the rigging called out whenever they saw drifting pack ice. The captain steered a zigzag course, full of abrupt turns.

Suddenly one of the sailors called, "Iceberg dead ahead!" Captain Sam leaped down from the bridge to help the officer at the wheel. Together the two forced the wheel all the way around. The ship veered and keeled sharply to one side. On deck, Mrs. Peary grabbed a post and held on to Marie. People slid past them. Marie squeezed her

huge stack of blankets on her little berth. She couldn't imagine needing them. But as the ship steamed northward Marie noticed that every day the air felt colder and the floating blocks of ice all around the ship seemed to be growing into towering masses. To Marie, the ice floes looked like white ships racing in the fast-flowing currents.

Icebergs off the coast of Greenland
(photo by Clarence Wyckoff)

eyes closed, sure they'd hit the iceberg and soon be killed. Slowly the ship began to right itself. Marie opened her eyes to see Captain Sam still grasping the wheel. The towering, jagged iceberg slid past the ship's side. They'd missed hitting it by inches. Before the giant iceberg was out of sight, they heard a deafening crash. The iceberg rolled like a whale and capsized, sending churning waters around the *Windward*.

The next day the fog lifted. A week later, the *Windward* entered Melville Bay, known as the Graveyard of Ships. Here, immense masses of drifting ice choked the Bay and locked the ship in ice for days. Surprisingly, Marie was allowed to disembark and play on the ice shelves. Mrs. Percy kept an eye on her while Marie pushed and glided on a sled made from two skis lashed together.

By mid-August, the captain announced they'd nearly reached the Inuit community of Etah on Smith Sound. Marie was so excited, she could hardly sleep—at last, after two years, she'd see her father. She remembered him as a "fur-clad giant" who gave her bear hugs. But when Marie and her mother arrived in Etah, they saw that Peary's U.S. flag was not hanging from the flagpole outside the red caboose that served as his little house—a sign that Peary was not there.

Captain Sam repeatedly sounded the ship's whistle. Marie watched as the Inuit rushed out of the skin tents clustered around the red caboose. Her fur-clad giant did not appear.

Fortunately, the captain found a letter from Peary tacked to the caboose's door. He'd gone to Payer Harbor, Cape Sabine on Ellesmere Island, three hundred miles north for the winter. Peary gave instructions for his supplies, stacked on the Etah beach, to be transported north along with the new stores carried by the *Windward*.

On shore, Marie and her mother explored the caboose, which seemed to Marie forlorn and dirty. She wished its red paint still looked new and shiny. Soon she and her mother were surrounded by Inuit, all excitedly talking and gesturing. To Marie's delight, she was greeted by Koodlooktoo. Marie also eventually met up with Billy Bah and Billy Bah's husband, Ahngoodloo. Marie hardly recognized Billy Bah, with her long tangled hair and fur garments, as the girl she'd known in Washington, D.C.

When the Inuit at Etah learned that the *Windward* was bound for Ellesmere Island, many asked if they could come along to hunt musk ox. Captain Sam agreed to take several families on the ship. Marie was excited at the prospect of the

A drawing of Peary's caboose by Russell Williams Porter

Inuit and their dogs coming on board and happy that Koodlooktoo was among them.

Once again, the *Windward* battled against the ice of Smith Sound. As soon as the captain forced a way between huge floes, the crew jumped into the rigging and chopped away the jagged points of ice that jutted over the deck. Though the captain had expected to cross Smith Sound in eight hours, the journey lasted eight days.

Finally, Marie and the passengers on the *Windward* reached the shelter of Cape Sabine's Payer Harbor—only to find that Peary had once again moved his camp. He'd gone north to Fort Conger. Inuit at Payer Harbor hadn't seen Peary in weeks and did not know when he would return.

Captain Sam explained to Mrs. Peary that he could not wait for her husband. It was now late August; he needed to return to Newfoundland immediately. In a few weeks the Arctic winter would set in, and Melville Bay would freeze over completely.

Despondent, Marie and her mother took their baths as usual in the ship's engine room and went to bed. Later that night, Marie woke in her berth to find her mother gently shaking her and the ship tilting on its side. Marie wrote, "When Mother saw that I was awake, she said: 'Get up, my lamb, and dress just as quickly as you can. I have laid your warm things out for you at the foot of your bunk. The Captain is afraid that he cannot save the ship.'"

Outside, a blizzard raged; during the night a

Josephine Peary, Marie, and Captain Sam Bartlett, 1901

sharp wind had driven the ship against rocks. Sailors rowed Marie and Mrs. Peary to shore through the blinding snowstorm. Once on land, Marie and her mother ran in place to keep from freezing while the exhausted sailors frantically unloaded the ship. They fastened lines around the masts and anchored them to rocks on shore in an attempt to prevent the ship from capsizing. As the ocean tide fell, the lines strained and creaked ominously.

Marie found a playmate on the beach, an Inuit girl called Achatingwah. Together they followed rabbit tracks in the snow, eventually coming upon an Arctic hare. Back at the beach, they found the sailors shouting. The tide had turned, and the *Windward* was righting itself. The ship would not be lost, after all.

Marie and Mrs. Peary were able to return on board for a hot breakfast. Water had poured in through their porthole and skylight, soaking their beds. Marie hardly cared. Soon the *Windward* was on its way again. But as the ship set course from Payer Harbor, they found the tide had stranded a huge mass of ice in the center of the narrow passage leading out.

The crew attacked the ice with saws and gunpowder. Finally, the sailors sought to blast it apart with dynamite. Still the mass did not move. Within days, water froze over in the harbor. They were trapped—prisoners of the ice. The long, intensely dark, and biting Arctic winter was upon them.

Marie and Mrs. Martha Percy in front of the ice-locked Windward

Chapter Five
Winter on the Ice-Locked Ship

Mrs. Peary and Captain Sam were worried about surviving the winter. For Marie, though, they were in the midst of an adventure. She looked forward to frequent visits on shore to see Kood-looktoo, Billy Bah, and Achatingwah. The sailors banked the ship with snow blocks and stretched a canvas tarpaulin over the deck. Marie found the space beneath a good shelter for running and playing games.

Mrs. Peary arranged for Inuit women to make winter clothes for herself and Marie. Each outfit featured a thick, hooded fox skin coat, or *kapetah*; warm sealskin boots, *kamiks*; and rabbit skin stockings. Marie loved dressing like her Inuit friends, although she wore heavy woolen underwear instead of a bird skin shirt, as they did. She couldn't get used to feathers next to her skin.

In September, Marie celebrated her seventh birthday. Her mother somehow found ingredients in the ship's supplies to bake a chocolate cake, and top it with seven candles. Mrs. Peary even produced a special birthday doll, one with long golden hair like Marie's.

As the days passed, Captain Sam recruited

In Inuit clothes, Marie, age seven, holds a narwhal tusk.

Inuit men to hunt for game in exchange for guns and ammunition. Mrs. Peary sent other parties of Inuit to look for her husband; they returned after two or three days, with Mrs. Peary's undelivered letters in hand. Meanwhile, the Etah Inuit families began work on their igloos, completing them just before the great Arctic night descended in October.

Marie helped Achatingwah's family build

their igloo. Later, in the dim light of the strong-smelling seal-blubber lamps, Marie and Achatingwah sat on piles of furs, making up stories and enacting adventures with small ivory figures. As the weeks passed, Marie taught Achatingwah English, while Achatingwah taught Marie to speak the Inuit language.

Every morning from ten o'clock to noon on board ship, Mrs. Peary tutored Marie. Part of Marie's lesson was to write an entry in her journal each day. She usually recorded the day's temperature, which could be as cold as forty degrees below zero Fahrenheit. Old Charlie prepared two daily meals: a breakfast of hot cereal with canned meat; and a midday dinner, often musk ox steak along with canned vegetables, bread and butter, dessert, and tea.

Many afternoons, Marie and her mother walked together in the moonlight. On the ship, they played Parcheesi or checkers and sometimes made taffy in the ship's galley. Before Marie went to bed, her mother sang her popular songs of the time, such as "The Old Folks at Home."

Sometimes when her mother sang, tears rolled down her cheeks. Marie assumed it was because the songs were sad. It didn't occur to her that her mother feared that her father could be ill or even dead. Many years later, Marie would learn of another of her mother's private griefs. Allakasingwah "Ally," the same young woman who sewed Marie's fur *kapetah*, was intimately involved with Peary. Allakasingwah's son,

Anaukaq, "Sammy," born the previous May, was Peary's son. Marie played with baby Sammy every day while her coat was being made, never knowing he was her own half brother.

That winter, Mrs. Peary reluctantly agreed to let Marie have a puppy. Cinnamon, or Cin for short, came from a litter of one of Achatingwah's father's dogs. Mrs. Peary joked that he should be named Sin instead because he chewed through mittens, ropes, boots, and anything else he got hold of on the *Windward*. At night, Cin joined in the howling of dogs on shore—a mournful sound to Marie.

Marie became a part of Inuit life. The Inuit loved stories and practical jokes. To Marie's

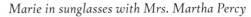

Marie in sunglasses with Mrs. Martha Percy

amusement, her friends frightened the gullible sailors with tales of ferocious polar bears. One day, after a heavy snowstorm, Marie came up with an idea to scare the sailors. Her sealskin boots made perfectly round footprints. With her fingers, Marie drew claw marks around each round footprint. Polar bear tracks! Enlisting the help of Koodlooktoo, Achatingwah, and other friends, Marie made "bear tracks" on the deck of the *Windward*, leading up to Old Charlie's galley. Sure enough, Old Charlie saw the tracks and bellowed: "[By] the Holy St. Denis! 'Tis a bear!"

The next day, the sailors refused to come out of their quarters. Finally Marie confessed the prank to her mother, who turned her over to stern Captain Sam. The captain brought her to the sailors' quarters, where Marie, trembling, told her story. Everyone was silent. Marie feared a terrible punishment. Then the men broke into laughter and gave her three cheers for keeping the ship lively.

It wasn't long before December came, and Mrs. Peary told Marie that there would be no exchange of Christmas gifts this year—there simply wasn't a way to have presents or a colorful tree and tasty baked goods as in past years. Marie pretended that she didn't mind.

Then, with several weeks left before Christmas, Marie and Koodlooktoo were sliding down a slope of ice. In the shadowy moonlight, Marie stepped off a shelf of the ice hill and fell ten feet. One of the crew members carried her, limp and

moaning, back to the ship. Marie lay semiconscious on her berth all night, crying over and over, "No Christmas! No Christmas!" In the morning, she announced to her mother that she was quite herself again, but ravenously hungry. As Marie ate, her mother said that perhaps there was a way they could celebrate Christmas, after all.

Marie spent the next two weeks helping her mother prepare for the holiday. Gathering treats from the gift baskets they'd received from friends before the voyage, they filled stockings for the sailors. Each stocking, made from white mosquito netting and tied with red cloth, contained chocolates, peanuts, dates, mixed candy, prunes, an orange, and a silver dollar. Marie and her mother popped corn, and Marie strung popcorn into garlands to decorate the main cabin. Out of canned milk and a powdered egg substitute, Mrs. Peary baked a whole stack of raisin cakes.

On Christmas Eve, Marie and Old Charlie served cake and hot chocolate to the crew. The next day, Marie awoke to find her own stocking filled with pink hair ribbons, a box of chocolates, watercolors, and a paper doll with paper dresses. That afternoon, another surprise awaited Marie in the main cabin: a small Christmas tree decked with candles twinkling gaily in the darkness. Mrs. Peary and the ship's taxidermist had made the tree from a broomstick and heavy wire. They'd covered the wire branches with softened wax and sprinkled it with coffee grains. For

A letter Marie wrote from the ice-locked Windward on February 21, 1901. However far Marie traveled, her thoughts remained with her family.

needles, they'd brought hay from old packing boxes. Marie wrote, "The result was so realistic that I imagined I could smell the balsam."

At the first full moon following Christmas, Marie and Koodlooktoo took a day trip together to Cape Sabine across the frozen bay, about four miles to the north of the ship. Captain Sam told them they were serving an important mission. He wanted a report on the condition of the ice at the Cape. It would help him judge, he said, how soon the ice in the bay would start to break up, so that he could make plans to sail.

Marie and Koodlooktoo trekked across the ice in the glittering moonlight and reached Cape Sabine without incident. As they ate their lunch seated atop a rocky hill, they scanned the view. To the north stretched unbroken ice fields. But when they turned to the south, in the direction they'd just come from, the ice had cracked into a channel of water, black and wide.

The roundabout route they had to travel back to the ship proved to be long and rough, up and down hills of ice and shadowy snowdrifts. At times they sank into snow up to their waists. Marie urged Koodlooktoo to stop for a rest. Koodlooktoo wisely insisted they press on. He knew that if they fell asleep they might freeze.

At last, from a hilltop, Marie saw the glowing lights of the *Windward*. Before her, or so it seemed, the hill stretched down into a smooth slope. Marie sat down on her bottom, preparing to slide. Koodlooktoo tried to stop her. He said the snowy slope was actually a glacier that could have a dangerous cliff. They should retrace their steps and approach the ship from the flat land.

Too tired to think clearly, Marie began to slide and soon picked up speed. The snow around her slid, too, and created an avalanche. Marie flung herself backward and stretched out her arms, trying to stop before the slope ended in an abrupt cliff that dropped down to the icy water below. But she kept sliding. Then, looking like a black bundle of fur, Koodlooktoo whizzed by her. Kicking and flailing his arms, he rolled almost to the edge of the cliff. He stopped and found footing. As Marie careened toward him, he shot out his arm and dragged her away from the edge.

Inch by inch, Marie and Koodlooktoo worked their way back up the hill and down the other side. Exhausted, they finally reached the ship.

There Old Charlie met them with steamy mugs of hot chocolate.

The rest of the winter passed less eventfully. To keep up their morale, Mrs. Peary and Marie celebrated every possible holiday or occasion— Valentine's Day, Lincoln's Birthday, Washington's Birthday, and Easter. Then, in March, the sunlight finally emerged.

By April the ice around the ship had mostly melted, and Marie needed a rowboat to visit her friends on shore. On May 5, Marie baked a cake for her father's birthday; Peary would turn forty-five on May 6. She supposed she and her mother would have to eat the cake without him.

Very early in the morning, however, Marie was awakened by a thud over her head, followed by the stamping of feet. Someone had jumped over the ship's rail and onto the deck. Mrs. Peary sat bolt upright in bed. Marie later wrote that her mother's eyes shone like two stars as she said, "It is your father!" The door burst open and Peary staggered in. He headed right for his wife. "I'm here, too, Dad!" Marie called excitedly. At last he took her into his arms. Peary joked that he'd smelled Marie's birthday cake and that's why he'd returned. In reality, he'd met a hunting party of Inuit from the *Windward* who let him know the ship was in the harbor. Sweaty and grimy, Peary excused himself to take a bath in the boiler room. Then, at five in the morning, Marie and her parents sat down to breakfast together for the first time in almost three years.

Marie eating dinner on the Windward *with her parents (on the far right) and members of the crew*
(photo by Louis Bement)

Chapter Six
Reunions and Farewells

It came as a bitter blow to Marie that her father would not be returning to America with her and her mother at the end of summer. Peary planned to stay in the Arctic for another year to try again for the North Pole. Marie would also have to say good-bye to Old Charlie, who'd decided to stay behind with the expedition. Still, Marie glowed with anticipation at spending the next three months at Payer Harbor with her father.

One morning Marie woke to see her father standing at the side of her bunk. He asked her to put her hand inside his coat pocket. Out came a grayish brown baby rabbit that Billy Bah had caught. Bunny, as Marie called him, came to live and play in Marie's cabin, sleeping in a box at night. Marie fed him fresh spring grass and willow shoots.

By early June, the ice around the *Windward* began to break apart, cracking with sounds like shattering glass. As the weather grew warmer, the sailors sawed at the ice hemming in the ship. At the same time, Billy Bah and Koodlooktoo took Marie to hunt for eider duck eggs on the steep ledges of a nearby island. Old Charlie cooked up some of them into scrambled eggs.

Marie reunited with her father in Payer Harbor, 1901

A storm in early July cleared the remaining ice from Payer Harbor. After ten months, the ship was free at last. Soon after July 4, the *Windward*, carrying the Pearys, expedition members and the regular crew, a large group of Inuit, and seventy-five dogs, left the harbor for Etah. From there the ship set out to sea again. According to a pact Peary had made with the Inuit, they would hunt walrus from the ship so the Inuit would have abundant meat to last them through the winter.

When the ship approached a group of several hundred of the large brown creatures sunning themselves on the ice floes, Marie went to her cabin to hide from the bloody slaughter. However, her father insisted she come on deck and watch; Peary wanted Marie to understand that hunting for food was a necessary part of Inuit life. The walrus carcasses were brought to ice floes for butchering. Despite the terrible odor and the sight of so much blood, Marie was fascinated by the Inuit men's skill as they cut and prepared the walrus.

After several days of hunting, the *Windward* headed back for Etah, and some of the Inuit disembarked. Others remained on board to return with Peary to Ellesmere Island. Peary had decided to spend the winter at nearby Cape Sabine. Yet shortly after leaving Etah's harbor, the ship once again became trapped by ice.

The *Windward* now carried ten Inuit families, forty dogs, and a bunch of yelping puppies, all crowded upon the deck. Some of the walrus meat began to rot, giving off a putrid odor. To relieve the monotony, Matt Henson initiated a day of relay races on the ice. Even Inuit women carrying babies in their hoods participated. Marie distributed the prizes of candy, sugar, biscuits, soap, and a mirror. The finale was a tug-of-war between the Inuit and the sailors.

During the tug-of-war, someone from the ship called out a warning. The flat ice where the games were taking place was cracking through the center. Just minutes after the crowd reached the safety of the deck, the thick ice floe broke into dozens of pieces.

Now the *Windward* could sail again. By nightfall the ship was safely anchored at Cape Sabine. In the following days, all supplies were unloaded onto shore. Peary supervised construction of a wooden house for his expedition members, and the Inuit built stone houses for themselves. The forward deckhouse of the *Windward* was set aside

A dogsled team. The wolf-like Eskimo Sled dogs, a breed similar to huskies, often fought with one another.

The Erik (left) arrives with fresh supplies to meet the Windward, *1901*

for Inuit women to sew fur garments for Peary's party. Marie admired her friend Billy Bah, who became known as the most talented seamstress of the group.

One day, the *Erik*, a relief ship sent by the Peary Arctic Club, entered Cape Sabine's harbor. Peary's main benefactor, Morris K. Jesup, had commissioned an expedition to find out what had happened to the *Windward* after it failed to return the previous year.

Marie and her mother eagerly opened letters and packages sent to them. They were comforted to learn that all their relatives in Washington, D.C., were fine. The Peary family moved their quarters to

Marie, nearly eight, at the helm of the Erik *(photo by Louis Bement)*

the *Erik*. It was a larger, cleaner, and sturdier ship than the *Windward*. The new cabin Marie shared with her parents was a small one, though, and they decided that Bunny would have to stay on deck.

Soon after the move, Marie discovered Bunny dead in his box. Marie suspected he'd been overfed by the sailors. She was devastated. She'd wanted so badly to see her brown rabbit turn white in the winter, to hold him and pet him, and show him to her friends in Washington, D.C. Adding to the sad loss of Bunny, Marie was feeling the pain of saying good-bye to her father, for the *Erik* was to set sail immediately.

Once back home in Washington, D.C., Marie, though she'd missed third grade, entered grade four. In spring, as the trees put out new leaves and the weather grew warmer, she eagerly anticipated voyaging north again to Greenland. In July 1902, when Marie was eight, she and her mother set sail on the *Windward*, captained once more by Sam Bartlett.

The ship arrived in early August at Cape York. Standing on deck, searching keenly through field glasses, Marie thought she'd spotted a large sled dog. Then she realized she was seeing white bearskin trousers. It was her father!

Marie soon learned her father had made another unsuccessful attempt to reach the Pole; but no matter, to Marie he would always be a hero. Indeed, Peary had traveled closer to the Pole than he'd ever done before. He'd reached 84 de-

Billy Bah, at age 16
(photo by Clarence Wyckoff)

*Achatingwah and
her baby, Anaukaq*

see Cin's two fat little puppies. Then Ahngood-loo, Billy Bah's husband, took Marie to a pen made from wire and boxes. Inside stood a woolly black musk ox calf. Old Charlie, who'd been feeding the orphaned calf condensed milk from a bottle, had named her Daisy.

grees 17 minutes north, a new "farthest north" record in the Western Hemisphere.

After Peary and Matt Henson boarded the *Windward,* the ship continued on to Cape Sabine to meet up with the other expedition members. There Billy Bah and other friends came on board. Achatingwah, who was twelve or thirteen, not only announced she was married but presented her newborn son, whom she carried in her hood.

After greetings were over, Marie asked her friends, "Where's Koodlooktoo?"

Achatingwah would only say, *"Tarangee!"* (Gone!) Marie feared that meant Koodlooktoo was dead. Soon she heard shouting. Through the field glasses, she caught sight of a sled team speedily bumping toward them down the glacier. It was Koodlooktoo!

Later, Koodlooktoo brought Marie ashore to

Charles Percy, Marie, and her pet musk ox, Daisy

Daisy became Marie's pet. Marie loved going along with Daisy as the ox kicked up her heels, bellowed, pawed the ground, and ran on the grass. Daisy's favorite trick, Marie wrote, was to come up behind her or Old Charlie when they least expected it and give them a little push.

After a few days, Peary's party headed back for Etah, where he had left some supplies. Peary was planning yet another expedition to the North Pole. Marie took Daisy on board the *Windward*, even though transporting her pet musk ox calf by rowboat, she wrote, was a "perfect circus."

Near Etah, Marie climbed the cliffs with Koodlooktoo as he caught little auks, small black birds. He would need their feathers for his winter shirt. Suddenly, a rumbling filled the air. Directly above them, the cliff began to crumble. Koodlooktoo and Marie, his arm sweeping her back, scrambled as far from the edge as they could go. The landslide thundered over them. When they returned to the ship, Peary heartily thanked Koodlooktoo for saving Marie's life. Peary presented him with a .44 caliber Winchester hunting rifle, a very practical gift, as a token of his respect.

Soon after this excitement, Marie and her parents—and Daisy—set off in the *Windward* for America. During the journey, Mrs. Peary broke the news to Marie that Daisy would not be coming home to live with them, but would go to a zoo in New York's Central Park. And there Daisy lived contentedly for a number of years. Though she grew large, as musk oxen do, when Marie came to visit, Daisy always recognized her friend.

Marie did not know when the familiar rocky shores and brilliant glaciers of Greenland slid astern that it would be twenty years before she'd see them again.

Chapter Seven
Eagle Island

In November 1902, nine-year-old Marie read in a newspaper, *The New York Herald*, that her father was preparing his next try for the Pole. Her father was fund-raising in New York at the time. Marie wrote him a letter from Washington, D.C.:

November 14, 1902

My dear, dear Father:

Of course I know the papers are not always right, but I read that the Peary Arctic Club are trying to get your consent to go north again. I think it is a dogs shame and wish every member of the Club were dead then you would not have to go in the first place. I know you will do what pleases Mother and me and that is to stay with us at home.

Robert E. Peary Jr. with his father in Bucksport, Maine, around 1904–1905

I have been looking at your pictures it seems ten years and I am sick of looking at them. I want to see my father. I don't want people to think me an orphan. Please think this over.

Your loving
Marie

As Marie well knew, there was no way of stopping her father's plans. He'd renewed his backers' confidence. In fact, President Theodore Roosevelt had arranged for Peary's latest promotion—he was now Commander Peary—and for Peary to take another paid leave from the Navy. Still, it would be several more years before Peary would depart for the Arctic. This time he'd build his own ship. So Marie's father did come home to live with his family. He gave Marie a bicycle as they celebrated Christmas together. But she still dreaded the day when he'd leave her again.

On August 29, 1903, Marie's mother gave birth to a son, Robert E. Peary Jr. The following year, the family moved to a newly built summer home on Eagle Island in Casco Bay, Maine.

As a high-school student, Peary had gone to Casco Bay on camping trips. Eagle Island was the spot he remembered most vividly. Peary called Eagle Island his Promised Land. Shortly after college, he'd purchased the island, and twenty years later, he built a house on it. The rocky bluff of the island looked to Peary like a ship, and the dwelling, which he set on the bare ledge of a steep cliff, he envisioned as the ship's pilothouse.

A postcard of Eagle Island and the Peary family's home.

could dress casually and swim at any hour of the day. Her mother's only rule was that she be clean for meals and at bedtime.

In the fall of 1904, after their first summer on Eagle Island, the Pearys moved from Washington, D.C., to spend a year in Bucksport, Maine. There, Peary could oversee the building of his ship, the *Roosevelt*. Named after President Theodore Roosevelt, it was the first ship built in America specifically designed for Arctic travel.

Peary journeyed each day to the shipyard in nearby Verona, where shipwrights were constructing the *Roosevelt* according to his instructions. It had three-foot-thick oak walls braced by steel supports, and a short, massive egg-shaped hull for easy maneuvering among ice floes. Marie often accompanied her father, and many years later recalled the smell of fragrant cedar chips from those days.

The house at first had three small rooms and one porch. Marie roamed in perfect freedom over the rugged and beautiful island—its steep cliffs, woods of white pines and chokecherries, and tide pools teeming with starfish, crabs, and sea urchins. Everywhere on the island pink foxgloves bloomed, and Marie's favorite flower, the morning glory, appeared in brilliant white or bright blue, twined around rocks and bushes. Marie

The Roosevelt *under construction. Robert E. Peary, second from left, stands with friends and supporters.*

From November to the springtime in Bucksport, Maine, the main mode of transportation was a horse-drawn sleigh. Getting about that way during the winter of 1904–1905, Marie later wrote, was travel she "enjoyed thoroughly, although I could never get the same thrill out of riding in a horse-drawn sleigh as I had out of riding with Koodlooktoo and his dog team."

In July 1905, Peary embarked from New York on his new journey. Mrs. Peary, Marie, now almost twelve, and nearly two-year-old Robert accompanied Peary on the *Roosevelt* steaming down the Hudson River. On shore, many people greeted them with flags and gun salutes as they passed. Marie and her mother and brother said their farewells to Peary before the ship headed out to sea. They steamed back to New York City on a tugboat, and Peary headed toward the Arctic. Newfoundlander Bob Bartlett, a nephew of Sam Bartlett, captained the *Roosevelt*. Though only thirty years old, Bob Bartlett was already well known for his ability to navigate Arctic waters.

Marie, her mother, and Robert spent their

Captain Bob A. Bartlett

summers on Eagle Island, and returned to Grossy's in Washington, D.C. each autumn. In October 1906, Peary came home, defeated once more by the brutal Arctic wilds—but having reached a new farthest north record of 87 degrees 6 minutes north. He'd now come within about 174 nautical miles of the Pole.

During this expedition Peary had achieved success with his new system of relay teams. But this journey was also marked by exhaustion, blizzards, and many other challenges.

In May or June of 1906, Ally, Peary's Inuit mistress, gave birth to Kali, a second son fathered

Marie and her family, 1905.
From left to right: Marie, age twelve;
Marie "Mayde" Diebitsch,
"Grossy" Magdelena Diebitsch,
Emil Diebitsch, Josephine Peary
holding Robert E. Peary Jr.,
and Robert E. Peary.

by Peary. Both Kali and his older brother, Anaukaq, were adopted and raised by Ally's husband, Peeahwahto. Fearing scandal, Peary never publicly acknowledged these sons. Nor would Marie ever speak of the matter when she learned of it many years later.

Peary returned to Washington, D.C., once again eager to raise funds for another Arctic trip. He traveled a great deal, and Marie did not see as much of him as she would have liked. In the fall of 1907, Mrs. Peary felt she wanted to help her husband with his lecture tour. Four-year-old Robert stayed with Grossy. Her parents thought Marie, who'd just turned fourteen, might be a bit too much of a tomboy and enrolled her in a girls' boarding school at the Visitation Convent in Georgetown, Washington, D.C. Separated from her mother for the first time, Marie spent a miserable year learning sewing and other "womanly" arts.

After school was out in June, Marie had only three weeks with her father. The family took a train to New York City. There they boarded the *Roosevelt*. With horns blasting, crowds cheering, and flags waving, the ship steamed up the East River. The date was July 6, 1908. The next day, while Marie and Robert Jr. stayed in the city with family friends, Commander and Mrs. Peary sailed to Oyster Bay, Long Island, to have lunch with President Theodore Roosevelt. The president was eager to see the ship named after him. He inspected its wooden hull and sturdy engines and greeted each crew member by name, finally giving his verdict: "Bully!"

At Sydney, Cape Breton Island in Nova Scotia, the family saw Peary off on what he promised would be his last venture for the Pole. He carried with him his wife's American flag and a sachet pillow Marie had filled with pine needles from Eagle Island.

In the fall, Marie, now fifteen, entered a public high school in Washington, D.C. She enjoyed it more than the convent school. Marie and a good friend at the school, Marguerite, attended their first dances. The following summer, along with her mother and brother, Marie returned to Eagle Island. She did not know when to expect her father. And she knew his quest could take his life and he might never return at all.

President Theodore Roosevelt wishes Peary luck on July 7, 1908, before Peary's final journey to try for the North Pole.

Chapter Eight
The Victory Tour

On the morning of September 6, 1909, Marie sat reading on the porch at Eagle Island. Over the water she heard the rumbling of a large motorboat. A man moored the boat, rowed to shore in a dingy, and ran up the front steps. Breathlessly he asked, "Is Mrs. Peary here?"

Marie answered that her mother was sleeping and should not be disturbed.

"I guess she will want to be disturbed by this, all right," the visitor replied, taking a telegram out of his pocket. "Commander Peary has discovered the North Pole!"

Marie excitedly yanked the man inside the house and hurried upstairs to her mother. Together they read the telegram: "To the Associated Press, New York City. Have nailed the Stars and Stripes to the Pole. Peary."

The New York Herald, *September 7, 1909. Marie, in the picture to the right of Peary wearing a hat trimmed with roses, turned sixteen the week this article was published. In the far right oval, Robert E. Peary Jr. holds a kitten.*

NEW YORK, TUESDAY, SEPTEMBER 7, 1909.—TWENTY-FOUR PAGES.— BY THE NEW YORK HERALD COMPANY.

ROBERT E. PEARY, AFTER 23 YEARS SIEGE, REACHES NORTH POLE; ADDS "THE BIG NAIL" TO NEW YORK YACHT CLUB'S TROPHIES; DR. COOK TO SUBMIT RECORDS TO UNIVERSITY OF DENMARK

ROBERT E. PEARY AND MRS PEARY ON BOARD THE HERALD DESPATCH BOAT OWLET JUST BEFORE HIS DEPARTURE FOR THE NORTH.

Discoverer of the Pole Joins in Cheering When Told Mr. Peary's Success

"If He Has Announced He Has Reached the Farthest North, He Has," Is the Physician's First Comment.

"THERE IS HONOR ENOUGH ON IT FOR BOTH OF US," HE ASSERTS TO ADMIRERS

THE ROOSEVELT LEAVING NEW YORK HARBOR

MISS MARIE A. PEARY DAUGHTER OF ROBERT E. PEARY

ROBERT E. PEARY, JR. WITH THE ROOSEVELT'S MASCOT

ROBERT E. PEARY

CAPTAIN "BOB" BARTLETT OF THE ROOSEVELT

Attains Highest Point on April 6, 1909, Year After Dr. Cook's Discovery

Sends First News of His Achievement from Indian Harbor via Cape Ray, on Newfoundland Coast.

FILES MESSAGES OF SUCCESS, THEN

Mrs. Peary doubted the message, feeling that if the news were true, she would have heard it directly from her husband.

Minutes later, a second boat approached the island bringing the personal cable to her. It said, "Have made good at last."

Soon more eager reporters docked at the island, though Marie and her mother were upstairs busily packing their bags. With Robert, now six, they boarded a train the next day from Portland, Maine, bound for Sydney, Nova Scotia, to meet the *Roosevelt*. Riding the same train were reporters, photographers, and scientists.

During the week, as everyone waited by the harbor for the *Roosevelt* to appear, Marie spoke often with the press. She gained the reporters' respect and affection for her enthusiasm, modesty, and interesting descriptions of the far north. On September 12, Marie's sixteenth birthday, journalists gave her red roses and a gold locket engraved with a map of Greenland. A star on the locket marked her birthplace.

Marie, her mother, and brother join Peary on the Roosevelt *in Sydney Harbor, Nova Scotia, September 1909*

The Roosevelt *with signal victory flags*

A few days later, word came to Mrs. Peary that the *Roosevelt* was steaming toward Sydney. In a yacht owned by family friends, Mrs. Peary, Marie, and Robert motored toward the ship. The sight of the *Roosevelt*, displaying all the bright colors of her signal flags, was one Marie would remember for the rest of her life. From the top of the mizzenmast flew a red, white, and blue flag with the words *North Pole*. Marie climbed onto the ship and embraced her father. She later wrote, "Every one was in wild spirits and Dad was here, there and everywhere, looking happier and prouder than I had ever seen him look."

Captain Bob Bartlett now artfully made his way around the many pleasure boats surrounding the *Roosevelt* as it neared Sydney Harbor. On land, a great crowd shouted and waved flags. A

A postcard of Frederick Cook

carriage escorted the Pearys to their hotel. Little girls ran alongside the carriage, tossing roses.

On every stop of the train returning to Portland, Maine, celebrations followed. Then, looking forward to the peace and quiet of their home, the Pearys went on to Eagle Island. But they were not alone, as eager reporters followed them.

A controversy erupted in the press. One story, told in banner headlines, was that Dr. Frederick Cook had reached the North Pole a full year before Peary. Enraged, Peary denounced Cook in several major newspapers, calling him a liar. Peary knew that Cook had been in Greenland. From talking to Inuit who'd seen Cook, Peary learned that Cook had set out on the Arctic ice in a party of only himself, two Inuit, and a single sledge that broke during their journey. Peary believed Cook missed the Pole by hundreds of miles.

But Dr. Cook had emerged from the Arctic region's snowstorms and ice five days before Peary. In that short time, he'd been hailed by the King of Denmark as a hero, even if he hadn't given proof to the scientific community. Peary

Dogs crowd the Roosevelt's deck. In addition to the noise and confusion of more than two hundred animals aboard, the ship had a choking stench.

knew that on returning to Eagle Island, his first task would be to organize evidence of his success to present to the scientific societies of the world.

Showing gratitude to his expedition members was important for Peary, too. En route from Nova Scotia to New York, the *Roosevelt* docked at Eagle Island. Peary invited the expedition members and ship's crew to a grand dinner. Marie took the now-famous expedition team of Matt Henson, Captain Bob Bartlett, Donald MacMillan, George Borup, and Dr. J. W. Goodsell on a tour of her beloved island.

Marie in turn listened raptly to the stories of their trek. After the *Roosevelt* had reached Cape York, Greenland, twenty-two Inuit men, seventeen Inuit women, ten Inuit children, and 226 dogs came on board. During the winter, the expedition team made clothes, built sledges, and readied navigation equipment and supplies for the journey. Unfortunately, the dogs' diet of whale meat went bad and eighty of the dogs died.

Peary followed the same route as his previous expedition. This time, however, he calculated allowances for the eastward drift of the polar ice. Peary and his team of five Americans, one Newfoundlander, seventeen Inuit men, and 133 dogs set out on the ice in March 1909, following four relay teams. The main team consisted of Peary, Henson, Captain Bartlett, and several Inuit. In the continuing daylight of the Arctic spring, the men traveled in twelve-hour stretches. Every few days, a team returned to base camp, reinforcing the trail and taking back the weakest dogs and any broken sledges for recovery and repair.

Again and again, as the weeks passed, the party hauled their sledges over jagged hills of ice and crossed treacherous lanes, or leads, of open water. These leads opened and closed with surf-like roars and dense clouds of vapor. Peary referred to the largest gap in the ice at different times in his writings as the Hudson River, the Big Lead, and finally the River Styx, after the

Peary's 1909 expedition experiencing favorable conditions on the ice

mythical river of death in Greek mythology. During the several-month journey, most, if not all, of the men fell into freezing water. It was the work, the Inuit said, of Tornarsuk, a troublesome spirit, who had plans to doom them for encroaching upon his domain.

Peary and his main team pushed on toward the Pole. As they neared the long-treasured goal, Peary picked a smaller and more streamlined group to make the final trek—133 miles. The team would be Peary, Matt Henson, and four Inuit: Egingwah, Seegloo, Ootah, and Ooqueah. They forged ahead with the forty strongest dogs on the five best sledges. Bartlett turned back to camp with his Inuit companions.

Peary reached 90 degrees north latitude—the North Pole—on April 6, 1909. On that morning, the six men built a towering cairn of ice blocks and placed Mrs. Peary's tattered flag at the apex. Peary enclosed a diagonal strip from the flag in a glass bottle along with two messages claiming the Pole for the United States and the Peary Expedition. To record their journey, they spent thirty hours taking measurements—sextant sightings— over a ten-mile radius. They took and posed for photographs. There were no landmarks to distinguish this place from any other on its surrounding polar sea.

When Peary's team reached the *Roosevelt* sixteen days later, they had to wait for the ice that locked the ship in place to melt. The ship was able to start southward on July 18. Peary brought the

Victory at the North Pole

Inuit back to their homes in the Etah and Cape York regions. His job was over, he told his invaluable companions. He wouldn't be sailing back to see them. After many years and journeying countless miles by sea, land, and ice, he'd finally accomplished what he'd set out to do.

The Peary family remained at Eagle Island until late October that year, when they returned to Washington, D.C. Marie began school nearly two months late. While the controversy over who had first reached the Pole continued, Peary submitted his journals and notes for review to several geographical and scientific societies. Among the first to endorse him was the National Geographic Society.

Many Americans remained skeptical that Peary had reached the Pole. But his many admirers in Europe were eager to congratulate him.

Marie and Robert were allowed to travel with their parents on a European tour the following spring. For the occasion, Mrs. Peary bought Marie her first fashionable party dress, which featured a low neckline and short sleeves. The Pearys boarded an ocean liner in April 1910, bound for England. Commander Peary was honored by geographical and scientific societies over the next two months; during this time Marie visited London, Berlin, Venice, Rome, Vienna, Budapest, and Edinburgh. She toured castles and palaces, rode through canals in a gondola, and was introduced to dukes and other royalty. She met many accomplished people, including Captain Robert Scott, the Antarctic explorer, and Robert Louis Stevenson, the author of *Treasure Island*.

As exciting as her trip to Europe had been,

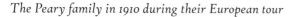

The Peary family in 1910 during their European tour

Marie was glad to board a liner in Southampton on June 11 to sail to America. Back on Eagle Island, her father hired contractors to expand their home. Using boulders from the shore, Peary designed a natural outdoor swimming pool for Marie and Robert; the pool enclosed the tidewater, which was heated by sunlight. In a woodworking shop with windows overlooking the bay, Marie and Robert each kept their own tools. Peary also built a shed for taxidermy, where he prepared a twenty-pound lobster for display in the dining room.

Peary tutored Robert in history and also made a list of books he felt Marie should read. Together they discussed them. Mrs. Peary planted roses, peonies, purple hydrangea bushes, leeks, and many other flowers and vegetables in a large garden. Marie and her mother gathered wild currants and raspberries and made them into jams. The family walked together through the fresh sea air and fragrant woods.

The controversy over whether Peary had reached the Pole ahead of anyone else continued for years. But to Marie, her father would always be the visionary explorer who was the very first to set foot on the North Pole. And best of all, at last he'd come home for good.

Marie once wrote of her childhood, "What girl could ask for more?" She loved her gallant father and lovely mother and the exciting journeys they'd taken to Greenland. Marie kept with her, pressed in a scrapbook, the purple, white, and

Josephine and Marie present Jo's flag to the National Geographic Society. Admiral Peary left a piece of this flag in every major destination; and later Jo added patches to commemorate his various landmarks. The diagonal band represents Peary's heroic 1909 trek to the North Pole.

yellow flowers that grew in spring in meadows near her birthplace.

Marie cherished the rugged sweep of the Arctic. She often thought of its rocks and expanses, its creaking and groaning glaciers, its icebergs shaped like palaces and ships. She remembered in dreams the barking of spotted seals and roars of walruses echoing over ice floes, the long-toothed narwhals, and shaggy dogs, as wild in spirit as wolves. She relived climbing up cliffs crowded with numberless noisy seabirds, the air alive with their spreading wings and calls. She felt the thrill of sliding on shimmering ice by the glow of the moon and stars during the long months of the Arctic night.

Even more than the northern landscape and animals, Marie loved the fur-clad Inuit, who carried their babies peeking out from their hoods. She remembered their graceful movements among the ice floes in skin kayaks and the way they excitedly moved their arms and laughed as they told stories.

From the time her mother first wrapped her in a caribou skin bag and an American flag and walked with her out of the lodge to see the brilliant world she was born into, the Arctic had become a part of Marie. She'd always be the child of its mysterious and magical vistas that inspired her name, Snow Baby.

Marie as a young woman

Afterword

The fiery debate over who had reached the Pole first has stayed alive to the present time. Most experts now agree that Cook did not get to the Pole; but a few noted scientists and explorers debate whether Peary's measurements were accurate enough to prove he did.

Marie, who turned sixteen the year of her father's legendary expedition, became known the world over. She toured Europe a second time with her family and studied French and German in Geneva, Switzerland, for a year. She attended secretarial school so she could help her father with his writings and speeches. In 1917, she married Washington attorney Edward Stafford and later gave birth to two sons, Edward and Peary Stafford.

After concluding his Arctic work in 1909, Admiral Robert E. Peary set himself the task of bringing aviation to popular awareness, mapping air routes, and educating the U.S. government about aviation's commercial and military potential. Working with the Aero Club of America, Peary gave hundreds of lectures across the country, and during World War I, he helped to create America's first air force. Marie worked closely with him in these pursuits as his personal secretary.

Peary's health, however, was failing. Suffering from pernicious anemia, which may have developed from vitamin deficiencies while he lived in the Arctic, he died on February 20, 1920, at the age of sixty-three.

After Peary's death, the family still summered on Eagle Island. Josephine Peary occasionally accepted invitations to lecture on the Arctic and championed her husband's accomplishments. As the first woman to participate in an Arctic expedition, she was honored by the National Geographic Society. Mrs. Peary died in 1955. The family gave Eagle Island to the state of Maine in 1967. The house and island are presently a state park and are open to visitors in the summer.

Robert E. Peary Jr. following his father's example, graduated from Bowdoin College, became a civil engineer, and made two trips to the Arctic as a young man. He married and had two children, settled in Maine, and enjoyed summers and even an occasional winter on Eagle Island. Robert E. Peary Jr. died in 1994 at the age of ninety.

Matthew Henson, Peary's indispensable partner in his Arctic expeditions, never gained due acknowledgment and fame for his achievements during his lifetime. After the great expedition of 1909, he settled into a modest job as messenger and clerk at the Customs House in New York City. In 1912, he published his autobiography, *A Black Explorer at the North Pole.* Henson died in 1955.

As for the Inuit of the Etah and Cape York re-

Marie's sons, Edward and Peary Stafford, in Greenland, 1932

gions of northern Greenland, after Peary's departure in 1909, they were left without the trade goods they'd grown accustomed to. These items, including guns, ammunition, wood, and sewing needles, were not essential to their survival, yet they had made their difficult lives easier. Fortunately, the Greenland Church established a mission base in northern Greenland in 1909, along with a trading post. This mission was part of a movement that saw Denmark take jurisdiction over North Greenland in stages over many years. Today several hundred Inuit live in North Greenland. They use cell phones and computers, and travel from their area to Denmark and other places for school and work. But many still sustain themselves by traditional hunting.

Marie's experiences and friendship with the Inuit during her childhood were precious to her. In her writings, she described her stays in Greenland as the happiest and most exciting times of her life. Her childhood experiences set the foundation for much of her later years when she wrote about and lectured on the Inuit and was active politically on their behalf.

In 1932, Marie finally was able to journey back to her birthplace and erect a memorial in honor of her father. Set on a promontory at Cape York, the giant three-sided tower serves as a navigational aid to the "Gateway of the North"—the first piece of land sighted when a ship approaches Greenland from America.

From time to time, Marie heard news of Inuit she'd known. Billy Bah married three times. Missionaries converted Koodlooktoo to Christianity. Sadly, before Marie returned to Greenland in 1932, most of the Inuit she knew had died, including Billy Bah, Koodlooktoo, and Achatingwah.

Later, during World War II, Marie served on a Danish-American commission that established security for Denmark and Greenland. For her efforts on behalf of the Inuit, the Danish government awarded Marie the Liberation Medal.

Marie's husband, Edward Stafford, died in 1955. In 1967 Marie married William Kuhne, a retired seaman.

Marie wrote many articles and five children's books: *The Red Caboose: With Peary in the Arctic; Discoverer of the North Pole: The Story of Robert E. Peary; Little Tooktoo: The Story of Santa Claus' Youngest Reindeer; Muskox, Little Tooktoo's Friend;* and *The Snowbaby's Own Story,* upon which this book is based. She was awarded an honorary Master of Arts degree from Bowdoin College.

Aside from these other accomplishments, Marie also completed the enormous task of organizing and cataloging her father's papers. She devoted ten years to this work before donating the papers to the National Archives.

Marie died in 1978 in Brunswick, Maine, at the age of eighty-five.

Marie Ahnighito Peary Stafford Kuhne in later years

Bibliography

Primary Sources:

Gillis, Kim Fairley and Silas Hibbard Ayer III, editors. *Boreal Ties: Photographs and Two Diaries of the 1901 Peary Relief Expedition*. Albuquerque: University of New Mexico Press, 2002.

Henson, Matthew A. *A Black Explorer at the North Pole*. New York: Walker, 1969.

Peary, Josephine Diebitsch. "Marie's Sayings and Doings." Unpublished manuscript. Josephine Diebitsch Peary Collection, Maine Women Writers Collection, University of New England, Portland, Maine.

———. *My Arctic Journal: A Year Among Ice-Fields and Eskimos*. New York: The Contemporary Publishing Co., 1893.

———. *The Snow Baby: A True Story With True Pictures*. New York: Frederick A. Stokes Company, 1939.

———. Unpublished diaries and letters. Josephine Diebitsch Peary Collection, Maine Women Writers Collection, University of New England, Portland, Maine.

Peary, Marie Ahnighito. *The Red Caboose: With Peary in the Arctic*. New York: William Morrow & Company, 1932.

———. *The Snowbaby's Own Story*. New York: Frederick A. Stokes Company, 1934.

Peary, Robert E. "First Report by Commander Robert E. Peary, U.S.N., September 6, 1909." *National Geographic*. (October 1909): 896–916.

———. "Nearest the Pole." *National Geographic*. (July 1907): 446–450.

———. *Nearest the Pole: A Narrative of the Polar Expedition of the Peary Arctic Club in the S.S. Roosevelt, 1905–1906*. New York: Doubleday, Page & Co., 1907.

———. *The North Pole: Its Discovery in 1909 Under the Auspices of the Peary Arctic Club*. New York: Frederick A. Stokes Company, 1910.

———. *Northward Over the "Great Ice," Volumes I and II*. New York: Frederick A. Stokes Company, 1898.

———. *Snowland Folk: The Eskimos, the Bears, the Dogs, the Musk Oxen, and Other Dwellers in the Frozen North*. New York: Frederick A. Stokes Company, 1904.

Stafford, Edward P. *Peary and His Promised Land: The Story of a Love Affair Between a Man and an Island*. Bailey Island, Maine: Friends of Peary's Eagle Island, 1998.

Stafford, Marie Peary. *Discoverer of the North Pole: The Story of Robert E. Peary*. New York: William Morrow & Company, 1959.

———. Unpublished diaries and letters. Marie Peary Stafford Kuhne Collection, Maine Women Writers Collection, University of New England, Portland, Maine.

Secondary Sources:

Anderson, Madelyn Klein. *Robert E. Peary and the Fight for the North Pole*. New York: Franklin Watts, 1992.

Bryan, C.D.B. *The National Geographic Society: 100 Years of Adventure and Discovery*. New York: Harry N. Abrams, 2001.

Calvert, Patricia. *Robert E. Peary*. New York: Benchmark Books, Marshall Cavendish, 2002.

Counter, S. Allen. *Polar Legacy: Black, White and Eskimo*. Amherst: University of Massachusetts Press, 1991.

Dolan, Edward. *Matthew Henson, Black Explorer*. New York: Dodd, Mead & Company, 1979.

Harper, Kenn. *Give Me My Father's Body: The Life of Minik, the New York Eskimo*. South Royalton, Vt.: Steerforth Press, 2000.

Herbert, Wally. "Commander Robert E. Peary: Did He Reach the Pole?" *National Geographic*. (September 1988): 387–413.

———. *The Noose of Laurels: Robert E. Peary and the Race to the North Pole*. New York: Atheneum, 1989.

Hobbs, William Herbert. *Peary*. New York: The Macmillan Company, 1936.

Lord, Walter. *Peary to the Pole*. New York: Harper & Row, 1963.

National Geographic Society. "Farthest North." *National Geographic*. (November 1906): 638–644.

———. "Peary on the North Pole." *National Geographic*. (January 1903): 29.

———. "Peary's Explorations in 1898–1899." *National Geographic*. (October 1899): 415–416.

———. "Peary's Work in 1900 and 1901." *National Geographic*. (October 1901): 357–361.

———. "Peary's Work in 1901–1902." *National Geographic*. (October 1902): 384–386.

Weems, John E. *Peary: The Explorer and the Man*. Boston: Houghton Mifflin, 1967.

Source Notes

Opening Quote

p. vi   "Whenever . . . that baby." Marie Ahnighito Peary, *The Snowbaby's Own Story*, p. 49.

Chapter One: The Snow Baby

p. 1   "She did this . . . husband." *The Snowbaby's Own Story*, p. 9.

p. 3   "When the earliest . . . toy." Robert E. Peary, *Northward Over the Great Ice, Volume II*, p. 69.

p. 5   "Will she . . . unhappy?" John E. Weems, *Peary: The Explorer and the Man*, p. 150.

Chapter Two: A Life of Contrasts

p. 6   "That was . . . change." *The Snowbaby's Own Story*, p. 47.

p. 7   "Luck was . . . him." Marie Peary Stafford, *Discoverer of the North Pole*, p. 76.

p. 8   "Her trunk . . . into it." Josephine Diebitsch Peary, *The Snow Baby*, p. 43.

Chapter Three: Moving the Iron Mountain

p. 14   "I can . . . Ahnighito." *The Snowbaby's Own Story*, p. 39.

p. 15   "to let . . . day." Ibid. p. 46.

Chapter Four: Adventures on the Windward

p. 16   "Keep smiling . . . you!" Ibid. p. 51.

p. 16   "marvelous plans . . . dolls." Ibid. p. 52.

pp. 16–17 "weather-beaten old fanatic." Wally Herbert, *The Noose of Laurels*, p. 152.

p. 17   "black sea monster." *The Snowbaby's Own Story*, p. 54.

p. 17   "Little Miss Peary . . . button." Jack Shanahan, a fireman on the *Windward* in an undated newspaper article in *The Daily News*, circa 1902. Josephine Diebitsch Peary Collection, Maine Women Writers Collection, University of New England, Portland, Maine, scrapbook 1, folder 39.

p. 18 "Iceberg dead ahead!" *The Snowbaby's Own Story*, p. 61.

p. 19 "fur-clad giant." Ibid. pp. 71–72.

p. 20 "When Mother . . . ship." Ibid. pp. 71–72.

Chapter Five: Winter on the Ice-Locked Ship

p. 24 "[By] the Holy . . . bear!" Ibid. p. 100.

p. 24 "No Christmas! No Christmas!" Ibid. p. 104.

p. 25 "The result . . . balsam." Ibid. p. 109.

p. 26 "It is your father!" Ibid. pp. 123–124.

p. 26 "I'm here, too, Dad!" Ibid. pp. 125.

Chapter Six: Reunions and Farewells

p. 33 "Where's Koodlooktoo?" Ibid. p. 169.

p. 34 "perfect circus." Ibid. p. 176.

Chapter Seven: Eagle Island

p. 35 "My dear . . . Marie." *The Noose of Laurels*, p. 151.

p. 37 "enjoyed thoroughly . . . team." *The Snowbaby's Own Story*, p. 219.

p. 38 "Bully!" *Peary: The Explorer and the Man*, p. 236.

Chapter Eight: The Victory Tour

p. 39 "Is Mrs. Peary here?"; "I guess . . . North Pole!"; "To the Associated . . . Peary." *The Snowbaby's Own Story*, p. 235.

p. 40 "Have made good at last." *The Noose of Laurels*, p. 282.

p. 40 "Every one was . . . look." *The Snowbaby's Own Story*, p. 238.

p. 44 "What girl . . . more?" Ibid. p. 54.

Acknowledgments and Picture Credits

Many thanks to Cally Gurley, curator, Maine Women Writers Collection, University of New England, Portland, Maine, for making the Josephine Diebitsch Peary and Marie Peary Stafford Kuhne Collections available to me. Mary Cresse completed my text and photo research at the Maine Women Writers Collection. My special thanks for help with additional photographs go to: Mimi Dornack, photo researcher at the National Geographic Image Collection; Kim Fairley Gillis; Nancy Hines, photographer, Classroom Support Services, University of Washington Libraries; Kate Philbrick; Alan Walker, archivist, National Archives; and Anne Witty, assistant curator, the Peary-MacMillan Arctic Museum, Bowdoin College. Mary Hillman, at the Lake City branch of the Seattle Public Library, arranged for me to see many rare books through interlibrary loans.

The following people read and commented upon the manuscript in draft form (any mistakes I acknowledge as my own): Dr. Susan A. Kaplan, director; Genevieve M. LeMoine, curator; and Anne Witty, all staff members at the Peary-MacMillan Arctic Museum; Dr. John D. Davis, vice president for education, The Friends of Peary's Eagle Island; Jeanie Dorrington, park ranger at Eagle Island; and Commander Edward P. Stafford, U.S. Navy (Ret.). Marguerite DeLaine served as the manuscript's fact-checker.

I'm most grateful for the inspired, skillful, and devoted editors who worked with the text at different stages: Peter Nelson, Julie Amper, and Mary Cash. Claire Counihan gave the book its design; and Kate and John Briggs con-

tinue to uphold my endeavors with cheer and goodwill. As always, I thank my community of writers who critiqued drafts—my Seattle writing group: Donna Bergman, Sylvie Hossack, and Suzanne Williams; and other wonderful writer friends: Stephanie Cowell, Mary Cresse, David Edwards, Jane Gardner, Elsa Okon Rael, Andrea Simon, and Sanna Stanley. Finally, there are those whose encouragement and counsel have kept me going through a long and labor-intensive journey: my husband, Jonathan Tait; my sister, Jennifer Kirkpatrick; my brother, Sidney Kirkpatrick; my agent, Liza Pulitzer Voges of Kirchoff/Wohlberg; friends Greta and Peter Nelson, and Liz Strausz. Heartfelt thanks to all.

The photographs and other illustrations in this book are used with permission and are herewith gratefully acknowledged:

American Museum of Natural History: pp. vi; 12; 36 (bottom)

Boreal Ties edited by Kim Fairley Gillis and Silas Hibbard Ayer III, photos courtesy of Kim Fairley Gillis and Silas Hibbard Ayer III: pp. 18 (bottom), 27, 30, 31, 32

Frederick A. Cook Collection, Library of Congress, courtesy of the Frederick A. Cook Society: LC-C752-125, p. 20

Josephine Diebitsch Peary Collection, Maine Women Writers Collection, University of New England, Portland, Maine: pp. 1 (bottom), 2 (top), 3 (top), 6 (bottom), 7, 9, 10, 11 (top), 16, 37 (bottom), 44

Library of Congress, Prints and Photographs Division: LC-USZ62-42993 p. 13 (top), LC-D4-39215 p. 40 (bottom)

Marie Peary Stafford Kuhne Collection, Maine Women Writers Collection, University of New England, Portland, Maine: pp. 25, 45 (bottom), 47

National Archives, Record Group 401, Russell W. Porter Papers: p. 19

Nearest the Pole by Robert E. Peary: pp. 17 (top), 33 (top)

New York Public Library: p. 39

The North Pole by Robert E. Peary: pp. ii, 18 (top), 29, 37 (top), 42, 43

Northward Over the "Great Ice" by Robert E. Peary: pp. 1 (top), 2 (bottom right), 3 (bottom), 5, 6 (top), 8, 14 (bottom)

Peary-MacMillan Arctic Museum: pp. 36 (top), 38, 40 (top), 41 (top), 45 (top left)

Robert Peary/National Geographic Image Collection: pp. 17 (bottom), 21, 23, 33 (bottom right), 41 (bottom)

Robert E. Peary and the Fight for the North Pole by Madelyn Klein Anderson: p. 35

The Snow Baby by Josephine Diebitsch Peary: pp. iii, 2 (top), 2 (bottom, left), 4 (top), 4 (bottom), 11 (bottom), 13 (bottom), 14 (top)

The Snowbaby's Own Story by Marie Ahnighito Peary: pp. 22, 28, 46

Index

Page numbers in italic type refer to illustrations.

Achatingwah, 20, 22–23, 24, 33, *33*, 47
Ahngoodloo, 19, 33
Ahnighito, 3–4
Allakasingwah, or Ally, 23, 37
American Museum of Natural History, 9, 11, 15
Anaukaq (Achatingwah's son), 33, *33*
Anaukaq Sammy (Ally's son), 23, 38
Anniversary Lodge, 1, *1*, 9, 14–15
Arctic winter (Great Night), 2, 2–3
   on ice-locked *Windward*, 21, 21–26

Bartlett, Bob A., 37, *37*, 40, 42, 43
Bartlett, Sam, 15, 17, 18, 19, 20, *20*, 22, 24, 25, 32
Billy Bah, or Eklayashoo, 4, 8, 12, 19, 22, 28, 30, 32, 33, 47
   in Washington, D.C., 5, 6–9, *6*
birthday celebrations, 15, 22, 40
Black Explorer at the North Pole, A (Henson), 46
Boas, Franz, 15
Borup, George, 42
Bowdoin Bay, 14
Bowdoin College, 7, 46, 47
Bunny (rabbit), 28, 32

Cape Sabine, 19, 20, 25, 29, 30, 33
Cape York, 32, 47
   meteorites found at, 5, 10–14, *14*, 15
Christian missionaries, 47
Christmas celebrations, 8–9, 24–25, 35
Cinnamon, or Cin (dog), 23, 33
Cook, Frederick, *41*, 41–42, 46
Cross, Susan J., 1

Daisy (musk ox), *33*, 33–34
Denmark, 47
Diebitsch, Emil (uncle), 7, *7*, 8, 9, 37
Diebitsch, "Grossy" Magdelena "Maria" (grandmother), 6, 7, *7*, 8–9, 37, *37*, 38
Diebitsch, Hans Herman, 7
Diebitsch, Marie or "Mayde" (aunt), 6, 7, *7*, 37
Diebitsch house, Washington, D.C., 6, *6*
dogs, *ii*, 2, 4, *4*, 5, 9, 10, 23, 29, *29*, 41, 42

Eagle Island, 35–36, *36*, 37, 38, 39, 41, 42, 43, 44, 46
Egingway, 43
Eklayashoo. *See* Billy Bah
Ellesmere Island, 19, 29
Erik, 30, *30*, *31*, 32
Etah, Greenland, 3, 10, 12, *12*, 19, 29, 34, 47

Falcon, 5, *5*, 6, 9
flag, U.S., 2, *2*, 14, 16, 19, 38, 43, *43*, 45, *45*

Goodsell, J. W., 42

Henson, Matthew "Matt," 4, 5, 9, 10, 12–13, *13*, 29, 33, 42, 43, 46
Hope, 11, 11–15, *13*, *14*

icebergs, 12, *18*, 18–19
igloos, 6, 22–23
Inuit, 1–2, 8, *8*, 11, 12–14, *13*, *14*, 19–20, 22–24, 28–30, 45, 47. *See also specific Inuit*
   brought to America, 5, 6, 6–7, *8*, 9, 15
   clothes of, 1, 3–4, 22, *22*
   in Peary's final push to North Pole, 42–43

Jessup, Morris K., 9, 16–17, *17*, 30

Kali, 37–38
Kite, 9
Koodlooktoo, or Nipsangwah, 4, *4*, 12, 13–14, 19, 20, 22, 24, 25–26, 28, 33, 34, 37, 47
Kuhne, William (husband), 47

Laura (nanny), 11–12
Lee, Hugh, 5, 9
Liberation Medal, 47

MacMillan, Donald, 42
Melville Bay, 13, 14, 19, 20
Meteorite Island, 13
meteorites, 5, 10–14, *14*, 15
Minik, 14, 15
musk oxen, 19, *33*, 33–34
My Arctic Journal (J. Peary), 3

National Geographic Society, 43, 46
New York Herald, 35, 39
Nipsangwah. *See* Koodlooktoo
North Pole:
   Cook's expedition to, 41–42, 46
   Peary's expeditions to, 4–5, 9, 16–17, 32–44, 34, 35, 38, 39, *39*, 43, 46

Ooqueah, 43
Ootah, 43

Payer Harbor, 19, 20–21, 28, *28*
Peary, Francine (sister), 16, *16*
Peary, Josephine "Jo" Diebitsch (mother), 6, 8, 9, 37, 38, 39–40, 44, 46
   in Arctic expeditions, 1–4, 5, 11, 12, 15, 16–28, 30–32, 34, 46

childbearing of, 1, 16, 35
courtship and marriage of, 7–8
death of, 46
photographs of, *iii*, *1*, *2*, *3*, *7*, *10*, *20*, *27*, *37*, *40*, *44*, *45*
Peary, Marie Ahnighito:
   birthplace of, 1, *1*, 14–15, 40, 45, 47
   marriages and childbearing of, 46, 47
   nicknamed "Snow Baby," 2, 45
   photographs of, *iii*, *vi*, *2*, *3*, *4*, *9*, *11*, *13*, *14*, *17*, *20*, *21*, *22*, *23*, *27*, *28*, *31*, *33*, *37*, *39*, *40*, *44*, *45*, *47*
   schooling of, 23, 32, 38, 43, 46
   writings of, 14, 47
Peary, Mary Wiley (grandmother), 7
Peary, Robert E. (father):
   Arctic expeditions of, 4–5, 8, 9, 10–15, 16–17, 19, 20, 26, 28–30, 32–44, 42, 46
   caboose of, 10, 19, *19*
   childhood and education of, 7
   courtship and marriage of, 7–8
   death of, 46
   fund-raising efforts of, 9, 10, 35, 38
   Greenland headquarters of, 1, 1–4, 19, *19*
   Inuit mistress and sons of, 23, 37–38
   lecture tours of, 10, 38
   photographs of, *1*, *27*, *28*, *35*, *36*, *37*, *38*, *39*, *40*, *44*
Peary, Robert E., Jr. (brother), 35, 37, 38, 40, 44, 46
   photographs of, *35*, *37*, *39*, *40*, *44*
Peary Arctic Club, 16, 17, 30, 35
Peeahwahto, 38
Percy, Charles "Old Charlie," 17, *18*, 23, 24, 26, 28, 33, *33*, 34
Percy, Martha, 17, 19, *21*, 23
polar bears, 10, 24
Porter, Russell Williams, *19*

Roosevelt, 36, *36*, 37, 38, 40, 40–41, *41*, 42
Roosevelt, Theodore, 35, 36, 38, *38*

Scott, Robert, 44
Seegloo, 43
Snowbaby's Own Story, The (M. Peary), 14
Stafford, Edward (husband), 46, 47
Stafford, Edward (son), 46, *46*, 47
Stafford, Peary (son), 46, *46*
Stevenson, Robert Louis, 44
Sydney Harbor, 40, *40*

Tornarsuk, 11, 43

walruses, 3, 4, 12, 28–29
Windward, 16–34, *17*, *27*, *30*
   ice-locked winter aboard, 21, 21–26, *25*